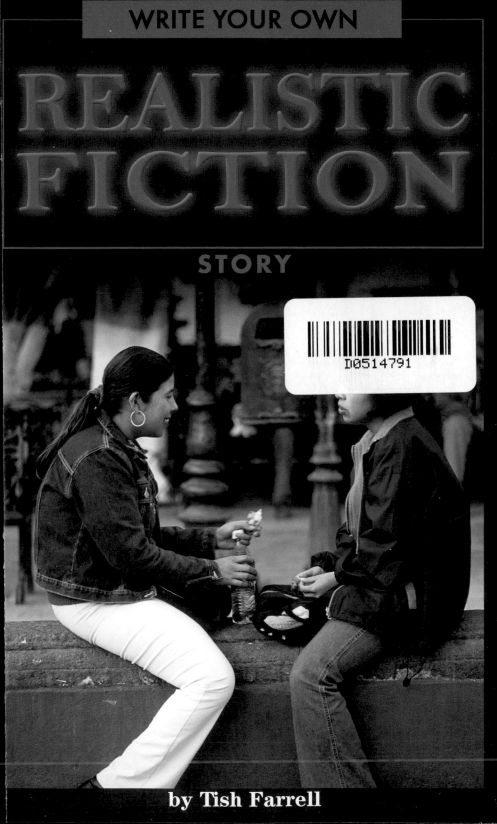

WRITE YOUR OWN

REALISTIC FICTION

STORY

D0514791

by Tish Farrell

First published in the United States in 2006 by
Compass Point Books
3109 West 50th Street #115
Minneapolis, MN 55410

Copyright © ticktock Entertainment Ltd 2006
First published in Great Britain in 2006 by ticktock Media Ltd.,
ISBN 1 86007 532 0 PB
A CIP catalogue record for this book is available from the British Library.
Visit Compass Point Books on the Internet at
www.compasspointbooks.com
or e-mail your request to
custserv@compasspointbooks.com

For Compass Point Books
Sue Vander Hook, Nick Healy, Anthony Wacholtz, Nathan Gassman, James Mackey,
Abbey Fitzgerald, Catherine Neitge, Keith Griffin, and Carol Jones

For ticktock Entertainment Ltd
Graham Rich, Elaine Wilkinson, John Lingham,
Suzy Kelly, Heather Scott, Jeremy Smith

Library of Congress Cataloging-in-Publication Data
Farrell, Tish.
    Write your own realistic fiction story / by Tish Farrell.
        p. cm.—(Write your own)
    Includes bibliographical references and index.
    Audience: Grade 4-6.
    ISBN 0-7565-1642-0 (hard cover)
    1. Fiction—Authorship—Juvenile literature. I. Title. II. Series.
PN3355.F37 2006
808.3—dc22   2005030731

Your creative calling

Do you want to tell exciting real-life stories? Is your creative mind transfixed by the social and emotional problems we all sometimes face? Would you like to write truthfully and accurately about what you see around you? This book will help you to write gripping realistic-fiction stories. To help you on your way, there will be brainstorming exercises that will develop your creative writing skills. There will also be hints from famous writers and examples from their books to inspire you.

ONTENTS

LEARN TO BE A WRITER

If you want to be a writer, this book is the perfect place to start. It aims to give you th tools to write your own realistic-fiction stories Learn how to craft believable characters, perfe plots, and satisfying beginnings, middles, and endings. Examples from famous books appear throughout, with tips and techniques from published authors to help you on your way.

Get the writing habit

Do timed and regular practice. Real writers learn to write even when they don't particularly feel like it.

Create a story-writing zone.

Keep a journal.

Keep a notebook—record interesting events and note how people behave and speak.

Generate ideas

Find a character whose story you want to tell. What is his or her problem?

Brainstorm to find out everything about your character.

Research settings, events, and other characters.

Get a mix of good and evil characters.

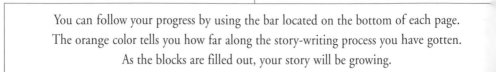

GETTING STARTED | SETTING THE SCENE | CHARACTERS | VIEWPOINT

You can follow your progress by using the bar located on the bottom of each page.
The orange color tells you how far along the story-writing process you have gotten.
As the blocks are filled out, your story will be growing.

Plan

What is your story about?

What happens?

A beginning, middle, and end.

Write a synopsis to create story-boards.

Write

Write the first draft, then put it aside for a while.

Check spelling and dialogue—does it flow?

Remove unnecessary words.

Does the story have a good title and satisfying ending?

Avoid clichés.

Publish

Write or print the final draft.

Always keep a copy for yourself.

Send your story to literary magazines, Internet writing sites, competitions, or school magazines.

SYNOPSES AND PLOTS · · · · · · · WINNING WORDS · · · · · · SCINTILLATING SPEECH · · · · · · HINTS AND TIPS · · · · · · THE NEXT STEP

When you get to the end of the bar, your book is ready to go! You are an author!

You now need to decide what to do with your book and what your next project should be.

Perhaps it will be a sequel to your story, or maybe something completely different.

CREATE A WRITING ATMOSPHERE

First gather your writing materials and find your story-making place. Writers are lucky. They can write wherever they please as long as they have a pen and paper. A computer can make writing quicker, but it is not essential.

What you need

The following materials will help you organize your thoughts as you learn your craft and do your research at the library or on the Internet:

- a small notebook that you carry everywhere
- pencils and pens with brightly colored ink

- different colored Post-it notes to mark any ideas during your research
- stick-on stars to highlight your best ideas
- folders for all bits of useful research and your brainstorming exercises to refer to later
- a dictionary, thesaurus, and encyclopedia.
- a computer or word processor

Find your writing place

Next you need to choose your writing place. Maybe it will be your bedroom or a spare room in the basement. Maybe it will be someplace public, like a library or a coffee shop. Author David Almond (*Kit's Wilderness*) writes on trains during his travels. Judy Blume (*Tales of a Fourth Grade Nothing*) has a writing cabin on an island.

Create a story-writing zone

• Play music that makes you feel calm and thoughtful

• Make a collection of striking images of people and places.

• Put on a hat or scarf that you only wear when you're writing.

• Choose some special objects to have around you while you work—a pen you use only for creative writing, a beautiful crystal to focus your thoughts, or a snow dome (to shake up your ideas).

Spend time choosing these things. Your writing place is important— special things are going to happen there.

Follow the writer's golden rule

Once you have chosen your writing space, the first step in becoming a writer is: Go there as often as possible and write. You must write and write regularly. This is the writer's golden rule.

Until you are ready, no writing can happen. It doesn't matter what you write—an e-mail or a diary entry will do—as long as you write something.

Before you can write captivating stories, you must begin training. Learning to write when you don't feel inspired is an important part of becoming a writer. To create the writing habit, good writers practice daily, just as an aspiring musician plays scales or an athlete does push-ups.

TIPS AND TECHNIQUES

Have a set time for your writing practice—10 minutes a day or an hour a week. Whatever you decide, make a date with your writing zone. Rain or shine, stick to your writing time.

Now it's your turn

Unlock your imagination

Begin your practice with some timed brainstorming to ignite your creativity. Have pen and scrap paper ready. Sit in your writing place, close your eyes, and take four deep breaths. Then write the phrase "Everything I've ever wanted to do" at the top of the paper. For two minutes, write anything that comes to mind. Go with your first thoughts. Let ideas flow like water from a fountain. Stop after two minutes. You're on your way to being a writer.

Now it's your turn

Burning ambitions

Run your eyes over your want-to-do list from the last exercise. Circle your favorite. Now imagine that you have your wish. For 10 minutes, brainstorm what you are doing and where. Write about how it feels to do it at last. Does your ideal pursuit have a special touch, taste, smell, sound, or look? Write only the first things that come into your mind. Don't worry about writing complete sentences. This is about becoming a writer, not being a perfect writer. When you have finished, give yourself a gold star.

The more you do exercises like these, the easier it will be to defeat the Story Saboteur— your internal critic who says your writing is useless. Try these storylines at practice time:

- *the day my house burned down and I became homeless*
- *my most embarrassing experience*
- *my best or worst birthday*

Case study

Louise Erdrich, author of The Birchbark House, wrote a lot as a child. Her father gave her a nickel for every story she wrote, and her mother made each story a wonderful cover. Erdrich says, "At an early age I felt myself to be a published author earning substantial royalties."

Good writing starts with lots of reading. You might choose to read realistic fiction about racism, running away, or what it's like to have a mother with purple hair. This genre includes many kinds of stories.

What is realistic fiction?

The thrills and tragedies of everyday living come into focus in realistic fiction. You can take on the issues that matter to everyone—from relationships with family and friends to struggles against poverty, discrimination, and illness. Whether it is comic or tragic, realistic fiction sends characters through many challenges, and your readers will learn something about life as your story pulls them along.

Read, read, read!

Read as many different kinds of realistic fiction as you can. This will help you to decide the kinds of stories you most want to write. Start an "ideas" file.

Look more deeply

Think carefully about the books you enjoy. Do you like the gritty drama of books such as Jerry Spinelli's *Maniac Magee* and Robert Cormier's *Heroes*? Or do you prefer Paula Danziger's wry humor in books such as *The Cat Ate My Gymsuit*? Reread one of your favorite books. Instead of losing yourself in it as the writer intended, imagine you are writing the story. Examine how the writer creates suspense, brings settings to life, and makes the characters seem real.

TIPS AND TECHNIQUES

The key to writing good realistic fiction is to tell a believable story from an unexpected angle. Use your own experiences and look to the heart of things as you write.

Case studies

Realistic fiction has long been popular. Louisa May Alcott's Little Women, *published in 1868, is based on her own impoverished family life. The book's straightforward style has made it a best seller ever since. Nineteenth-century author Charles Dickens also knew all about hard times. His own father was sent to a debtor's prison, and the writer used these experiences when he wrote* Little Dorrit. *After leaving school, Dickens worked for a law firm, recording court proceedings, and then as a journalist. He had the best possible practice for becoming one of his time's greatest writers of realistic fiction.*

Now it's your turn

Making real life magic

Imagine you are in charge of organizing a family gathering—a birthday party or a religious celebration—but you have no money to spend. Take 10 minutes to describe what you will do to make it special for everyone. Jot down your first thoughts.

To be a good writer you need to read with attention. This will help you to discover your own writer's voice—a style of writing uniquely yours. But it will take time. Many writers continue developing their voice all their lives.

Find your writer's voice

Read as widely as possible. Experiment. Try some different genres—or types of stories. A science-fiction or historical novel might give you some new ideas about storytelling. Don't forget to read poetry, too. Once you start reading as a writer, you will see that every writer has his or her own rhythm, style, and range of vocabulary. These remain consistent throughout each book. For instance, *Because of Winn-Dixie* author Kate DiCamillo sounds very different from *Maniac Magee* author Jerry Spinelli.

Now it's your turn

Personal experiences

Read the excerpts on the next page and copy the one you like best. Does the piece remind you of something that happened to you? If it does, write down your own story. Try writing it in a humorous style, and then in a tragic or sarcastic one.

DIFFERENT WRITERS, DIFFERENT VOICES

Look at the words these authors use. Think about the rhythm and length of sentences. Which style do you prefer?

Dodie Smith

I Capture the Castle *opens with an unusual beginning that establishes the story's voice:*

> *I write this sitting in the kitchen sink. That is, my feet are in it; the rest of me is on the draining-board, which I have padded with our dog's blanket and the tea-cosy. I can't say that I am really comfortable … but this is the only part of the kitchen where there is any daylight left. And I have found that sitting in a place that you have never sat before can be inspiring—I wrote my very best poem while sitting on the hen-house.*
>
> Dodie Smith, *I Capture the Castle*

Judy Blume

In Tales of a Fourth Grade Nothing, *Peter puts up with his brother Fudge:*

> *I finally got to bed at ten. Fudge was in his crib slurping away. I thought I'd never fall asleep! But I guess I did. I woke up once, when Fudge started babbling. He said, "Boo-ba-mum-mum-ha-ba-shi." Whatever that means. I didn't even get scared. I whispered, "Shut up!" And he did.*
> *Early the next morning I felt something funny on my arm. At first I didn't wake up. I just felt this little tickle. I thought it was part of my dream. But then I had the feeling somebody was staring at me. So I opened my eyes.*
>
> Judy Blume, *Tales of a Fourth Grade Nothing*

Sharon Creech

In Heartbeat, *Annie tells the story of her life in poems:*

> *Sometimes when I am running a boy appears like my sideways shadow from the trees he emerges running falling into thump-thump steps beside me.*
>
> Sharon Creech, *Heartbeat*

Stories rarely drop into the writer's mind fully formed. They begin with one or two ideas, which the writer then must research and develop. But where do writers get their ideas in the first place? There are many different sources out there.

Story of your life?

As you have seen, many famous writers use their own life experiences to write their fiction. This is a good way to start. If you write about what you know and feel and have seen, you will have plenty of good raw material for crafting believable settings and characters.

Start by keeping a diary

Before you say, "Nothing interesting ever happens to me," remember your burning ambitions. If nothing happened today, write about your hopes and dreams. Put a reminder in your diary or notebook: "Everything in my life is special in some way: I only have to look."

TIPS AND TECHNIQUES

Say you want to turn the details of a school camping trip into a story. First, think who your main character will be. It could be the shy class weakling. How does he stop being a victim and become a hero?

Now it's your turn

Decide what happens next

Using the class weakling as the main character, decide what will happen in your camping story. Will your character be ambushed by bullies and left dangling upside down from a tree? Finish the story in your notebook. Asking questions will help you shape the plot. What if your hero decided to fight back? How would he do it? What are the bullies' weaknesses? Who will help your hero?

Consider story subjects

Life is full of the makings of good realistic fiction: winning a big game, getting bad grades, training for a team, learning new skills, a family party, a bad day at school, the school trip, embarrassing moments, a camping expedition, foreign travel, an argument with your best friend, a hospital visit, cleaning out your grandma's attic, an issue you care about deeply. What else is on your list?

Making fiction from fact

Your diary entries will become your raw materials. They will have plenty of insights, but to make a good story with a believable hero out of them, you may have to exaggerate or alter events.

TIPS AND TECHNIQUES

Read some real-life diaries. **Thura's Diary** *is the account of a young girl's life in war-torn Baghdad by Thura Al-Windawi. Also try fictional diary stories like Sharon Creech's* **Absolutely Normal Chaos** *or Sue Townsend's* **The Secret Diary of Adrian Mole, Aged 13 3/4.**

Writing from firsthand experience is hard to beat, but if you want to write about someone whose life you've only glimpsed, serious research might be needed to make your story believable. If you are interested in your story's subject, research can be fun.

Star attraction

Suppose you want to write a story about a young movie or rock star. Begin by reading about as many real child stars as possible—Britney Spears or Macaulay Culkin (right), for example. Research stars from long-past eras, too, such as Shirley Temple and Judy Garland.

TIPS AND TECHNIQUES

Start a newspaper-clippings file of intriguing stories. Collect the most dramatic stories (such as kids who have won despite all the odds) and cut out photos of interesting characters.

Gather information

Collect articles from celebrity magazines and newspapers. Look at stars' official sites on the Internet. Make notes on what they say about themselves and how they live. Write down the actual words they use.

Now it's your turn

A perfect recipe?

Cut scrap paper into 80 pieces shaped like playing cards and divide them into four equal piles. Take five minutes to brainstorm ideas for each pile. You'll need 20 characters, 20 locations, 20 objects, and 20 actions. Shuffle the piles and deal yourself one card from each pile. You now have four basic ingredients to make a story. For 10 minutes, brainstorm your first thoughts about how they might come together and what happens.

Build a fictional star's profile

Build up a celebrity profile based on several stars' lives. If you do your research well, you will find all the real-life conflict and drama you need to make an interesting story.

Questions lead to stories

Ask questions and more questions to find your story. What are a young star's problems? Does he or she worry about appearance and develop an eating disorder? Does the star long for a true friend or want a different career? Asking questions will help you to see your character's story.

Case study

Jack Gantos created the Joey Pigza trilogy after meeting children with attention-deficit/hyperactivity disorder while visiting schools. One night, he was writing about a particular boy in his diary, and the character of Joey Pigza started coming to life. Gantos was inspired to write a story to show that children whose lives are managed by "meds" are not bad kids.

SET THE STAGE

In realistic fiction, the setting will play a big part in how everyone behaves, be it a war zone or the city streets. To tell a convincing tale, you will need to understand how the setting operates.

Exciting places

Don't bore readers by describing absolutely everything about your physical location. But make sure you know how the location will influence the human story. Again, this may call for research. Imagine you're doing a geography assignment; look for details on human settlement patterns, climate, natural history, communications, or emergency services. Sketching setting details will help you to understand them better. Choose the most dramatic features to use in your story. There are are several ways to make the setting work hard for your story.

Blend setting and action

In Gary Paulsen's *The Foxman*, the setting comes to life without using a lot of visual description. Instead, the author focuses on action and sound:

> *When you're alone in the brush and suddenly find yourself stone-blind, panic is the first thing that comes to mind. ... I crashed through the brush like a crazy man. Or maybe I should say I tried to, because I ran into trees and got knocked down and I'd get up and try again and get knocked down again. ... And then the sounds came. Things I'd never heard before, or hadn't noticed because I could see; little cracks and creaks from the brush, all sounding like something coming towards me. Maybe wolves and even knowing that wolves aren't that bad, don't bother people, my mind started working on how they could come in and tear me to pieces because I couldn't see to stop them.*
> Gary Paulsen, *The Foxman*

Now it's your turn

Get a sense of place

Go back to the chance concoctions you created with your set of story cards (see page 16). Think about the "character" and "place" that you dealt from your cards. For 10 minutes, write a scene that describes your chosen place from the character's point of view. Imagine your character is upset (decide why first) and find ways to reflect this in your description. Take a break and then repeat the exercise, but this time write to reflect a positive feeling—joy, relief, or hope.

Use setting to reveal character

At the start of Sharon Creech's *Walk Two Moons*, Salamanca is shocked when her father insists they move from their Kentucky farm to a small house in town. What does her description of her new home reveal about her feelings?

Tiny, squirt trees. Little birdhouses in a row— and one of those birdhouses was ours. No swimming hole, no barn, no cows, no chickens, no pigs ...

"Let's take a tour," my father said, rather too heartily.

We walked through the tiny living room into the miniature kitchen and upstairs into ... my pocket- sized bedroom.

Sharon Creech, *Walk Two Moons*

TIPS AND TECHNIQUES

When setting any scene, think of ways to trigger the senses. How does it smell, feel, sound, taste, and look from inside your own skin? Also keep thinking: How does it affect my characters and their actions?

WRITE ABOUT PEOPLE'S PROBLEMS

Realistic-fiction writers mostly write about human problems—such as being ill, losing a parent, coping with emotions such as jealousy and fear, or being bullied. The focus is on how the characters deal with tough problems.

Use humor

Seeing the funny side of the worst situations is a real gift. Writers like Jack Gantos, Sharon Creech, and Jacqueline Wilson are masters at using humor when relating sad events. They do not make light of issues by doing this. They present them in such an entertaining or uplifting way that readers cannot put their books down.

Present tragedy and hope

No one wants to read a book that makes them feel utterly miserable, so don't be too grim— even if you are writing a war story, you can include moments of hope and happiness. Authors often aim to give readers hope that even life's worst tragedies can be overcome.

Make a story frame

One way to make realistic stories special is to take an idea inspired by your story's main theme and weave it through the story like the chorus of a memorable pop song. In fiction, one object or idea can come back again and again, acting like a frame for the rest of the story. This isn't as complicated as it sounds. Here are some examples:

The tattooed mother

The Illustrated Mum is about a mother's mental illness and its effect on her two daughters, Dolphin and Star. Jacqueline Wilson shows us Marigold's illness through her obsession with tattoos. There is humor as well as sympathy. Each chapter relates to one of the tattoos. In this case (right), the tattoo is a serpent:

Marigold was knuckling her forehead, trying to ease a headache. Then she saw Star's empty bed and stopped dead, her arm still raised. She didn't say anything. She just lay down on Star's bed and started crying. These were new horrible heart-broken tears, as if she were choking. It sounded as if her serpent had coiled itself right round her neck.

Jacqueline Wilson, *The Illustrated Mum*

A dog changes everything

A stray dog creates the frame for Kate DiCamillo's *Because of Winn-Dixie*. The story is about a girl who has lost her mother and whose preacher father feels alone and isolated. The dog brings them and many other lonely people together:

Winn-Dixie looked up at the preacher ... wagged his tail and knocked some of the preacher's papers off the table. Then he sneezed and some more papers fluttered to the floor.

"What did you call this dog?" the preacher asked.

"Winn-Dixie," I whispered. I was afraid to say anything too loud. I could see that Winn-Dixie was having a good effect on the preacher. He was making him poke his head out of his shell.

Kate DiCamillo, *Because of Winn-Dixie*

DISCOVER YOUR HERO

Your hero is the lead actor in your story. You must care about him or her deeply and make readers care, too. Think of the character— who must be as real as possible—as a best friend or family member. Or perhaps your hero is based on you?

Give your hero problems

Stories about people with totally happy lives are very boring. Phyllis Reynolds Naylor's *Shiloh Season* begins, "After Shiloh came to live with us, two things happened. One started out bad and ended good. The other started out good and … Well, let me tell it the way it was." The more challenges a character has to face, the more fascinating they are to read about. In other words, readers are only interested in seeing how other people deal with their problems.

Find your hero

Writers find their ideas for leading characters in all sorts of ways—in newspapers, on the beach, in a TV documentary, or when some little thing triggers a memory of someone they once knew. The trick is to keep a lookout for ideas.

Build the picture

Think about what your hero looks like and what he or she likes and dislikes and is good at. What are your character's flaws and weaknesses? These can add more drama to the unfolding dilemma. Now focus on your hero's main problems. What is the history? What is happening now? In this example (right), Joey Pigza describes what it's like to suffer from attention-deficit/hyperactivity disorder:

At school they say I'm wired bad, or wired mad, or wired sad, or wired glad, depending on my mood and what teacher has ended up with me. But there is no doubt about it, I'm wired.

This year was no different. When I started out all the days there looked about the same. In the morning I'd be OK and follow along in class. But after lunch, when my meds had worn down, it was nothing but trouble for me.

Jack Gantos, *Joey Pigza Swallowed the Key*

Now it's your turn

In their shoes

For 10 minutes, put on your hero's shoes. Think about his or her weaknesses—perhaps a wild imagination, a fear of conflict, or a hot temper. Think of the good points, too—a sense of humor, a caring nature, or a willingness to stand up for others. Even good traits could get your character into trouble.

CREATE YOUR VILLAIN

There may be human villains in realistic fiction, but often the main villain may actually not be a person but the hero's bad situation—being on medication, dealing with a mother's mental illness, or grieving for a lost parent.

Bad guys

Just as in real life, there are people who behave badly in realistic fiction. They won't be evil in the way that fantasy or science fiction villains might be, but they can sometimes be terrifying. In *Shiloh*, Marty has to face Judd Travers, the cruel man who mistreats his dogs and wants to take Shiloh from Marty.

> *"Dogs okay?" Dad asks, and I know he's asking for me.*
>
> *"Lean and mean," says Judd. "Keep 'em half starved, they'll hunt better … lose one, I'll buy another."*
> Phyllis Reynolds Naylor, *Shiloh*

Misunderstandings

In Katherine Paterson's *Bridge to Terabithia*, Jess doesn't like Leslie when they first meet. Leslie has short hair and dresses like a boy, and even though her family has more money than Jess's, they don't own a television. Because she is different, Jess is sure that he doesn't want to be friends with her. The story then follows the growth of this relationship to a tragic conclusion.

Recovery

In *Face* by Benjamin Zephaniah, Martin has everything he wants and a lovely girlfriend, Natalie. Then there is a car crash. Martin wakes up in hospital with terrible burns. He has to learn to face his schoolmates' shock and horror. And what will Natalie think of him now?

Revenge

The main character in Louise Fitzhugh's *Harriet the Spy* writes down everything she thinks and sees, even if it's not very nice. She has never been caught … until the day her classmates find her notebook and read what's inside. Suddenly, Harriet finds herself with no friends and facing The Spy Catcher Club. She feels humiliated and begins to think of ways to get revenge.

TIPS AND TECHNIQUES

Don't make your bad guys all bad; maybe they are just behaving badly, but they have a better side. Maybe they are mostly rotten but capable of surprising kindness.

DEVELOP A SUPPORTING CAST

Even the loneliest hero must have supporting characters to interact with. Through others, we learn what your hero is really like—by seeing how he or she treats parents, friends, strangers, stray dogs, or enemies.

A good friend

The hero's closest friends are likely to be written in great detail. Find ways to make them interesting. In *Walk Two Moons*, Phoebe is an instant source of mystery for the main character, Salamanca:

> *I saw the face pressed up against an upstairs window next door. It was a girl's round face, and it looked afraid. I didn't know it then, but that face belonged to Phoebe Winterbottom, the girl who had a powerful imagination, who would become my friend, and who would have all those peculiar things happen to her.*
>
> *Phoebe was a quiet girl. She stayed mostly by herself and seemed quite shy.*
>
> Sharon Creech, *Walk Two Moons*

As we get to know Phoebe, we also find out that she makes surprising revelations, which no one quite believes. The function of Phoebe's story in *Walk Two Moons* is to bring us to the painful truth of Salamanca's own story. It deepens our understanding of what it is like when a mother leaves home.

Now it's your turn

Your hero's friend

Think about the main character you chose from the cards you made (see page 16). Who is this character's best friend likely to be? What is he or she named? How do the friends meet? Are they the same age? What kind of relationship do they have? Maybe they started off on the wrong foot. Take 10 minutes to brainstorm your first thoughts.

A silent partner

Sometimes the supporting characters aren't even alive, but they still do an important job of letting us hear the hero's thoughts. In Paula Danziger's *Amber Brown Sees Red*, we hear Amber telling her stuffed toy gorilla her worries about being split between her divorced parents:

The hairy ape still says nothing.

I get mad at him. "You don't understand. There's only one of you. What am I going to do when I go to Dad's and I need to talk to you and you're here? I can't carry you back and forth, take you to school with me. It would look really dumb for me, a fourth grader, to take a dumb stuffed animal to school."

Paula Danziger, *Amber Brown Sees Red*

TIPS AND TECHNIQUES

Use scenes with supporting characters to show your hero's strengths and weaknesses. Readers can learn a lot by seeing your hero tell a joke or have a temper tantrum.

CHOOSE A POINT OF VIEW

Who will tell your story—just one person or lots of characters? How much do you want your readers to know about all the characters? You will answer these questions when you choose a point of view (POV).

The omniscient

Traditional stories and many new ones, such as Jerry Spinelli's *Maniac Magee,* are written using the omniscient—or, "all-seeing"—view. The narrator describes all the characters and tells us what they think and feel. Here Spinelli describes the reaction in town to Jeffrey "Maniac" Magee's heroic feats that keep Russell and Piper McNab going to school:

> *To much of the town, hearing about these things, it was simply a case of the legend adding to itself, doing what legends do. To Russell and Piper McNab, it was a case of boosting their importance even higher in the eyes of the other kids. As for Maniac, he understood early on that he was being used for the greater glory of Piper and Russell.*

Jerry Spinelli, *Maniac Magee*

Now it's your turn

Switching viewpoints

Write a short scene in which two or more characters do something exciting like climb a mountain. First write it from the omniscient viewpoint, describing what all the characters do and feel. Then write it in the third person, giving only your hero's viewpoint. Finally, write it in the first person as if you are the hero.

The first person

The first-person viewpoint uses a character as the narrator of the story. The narrator can say, "I thought this" or "I did that." First-person POV is an exciting way to tell a story, but to be convincing you must know your character inside out. Every word must suit the character of your narrator. You can also use this viewpoint in letters, e-mails, or diary entries to add variety and interest to third-person narratives.

My life is not easy. I know I'm not poor. Nobody beats me. I have clothes to wear, my own room, a stereo, a T.V. and a push-button phone. Sometimes I feel guilty being so miserable, but middle-class kids have problems too.

Paula Danziger, *The Cat Ate My Gymsuit*

The third person

Another way to write a story is to tell it from the point of view of the main character but not in his or her own words. In third-person POV, the narrator observes the main character and can even know his or her thoughts. This viewpoint is usually written in the past tense:

How could he explain it in a way Leslie would understand, how he yearned to reach out and capture the quivering lie about him and how when he tried, it slipped past his fingertips, leaving a dry fossil upon the page?

Katherine Paterson,
Bridge to Terabithia

TELL YOUR STORY'S STORY

As your story starts simmering in your mind, it helps to write a few paragraphs about it. This is called a synopsis. It will keep you focused on your story's main theme and plot.

A good way to learn how to write a sharp synopsis is to study the information—called the blurb—on the back of a book. See how it makes readers want to find out what happens next. A good blurb provides a brief summary of the story and explains the characters. It also gives the tone of the book—serious or humorous—without giving away the ending. Here is the back cover text from Gary Paulsen's *The Foxman*:

"No one knows the Foxman is even there until Carl and his cousin stumble upon his shack deep in the woods. He doesn't say his name or show his face—it is hidden behind a mask—but he gives the lost boys food and shelter for the night. Carl is happy to leave the next day—having caught a glimpse of the Foxman's hideously mutilated face. But his cousin, a loner himself, will come back."

The blurb for *Maniac Magee* by Jerry Spinelli presents the situation of the story, which features a main character whose life has been transformed by tragedy:

"He wasn't born with the name Maniac Magee. He came into this world named Jeffrey Lionel Magee, but when his parents died and his life changed, so did his name. And Maniac Magee became a legend."

Now it's your turn

Write your blurb

Think about the focus of your story, which could be anything from a skater dude facing new competition to a teenage girl being shunned by her classmates. Try to sum up the story in a single striking sentence. Then give a glimpse of the main character's problem and the plot in no more than three brief paragraphs.

TIPS AND TECHNIQUES

If you can't sum up your story as simply as a blurb, it may be too complicated. Simplify it. As you work on your own synopsis and story map, ask yourself: Whose story is this and what scenes do I need to tell it? Think about your theme, too. In realistic stories this is usually a human problem—illness, dealing with loss, bullying, family troubles—and how the hero overcomes his or her difficulties to gain a better life.

Make a story map

You have a synopsis, a cast of characters, and a setting, and you've decided on the point of view. The next useful tool is a story map. Before filmmakers start filming, they map out the plot in a series of sketches called storyboards. This helps them to work out how best to shoot each scene. You can do this for your story. Draw the main events in pictures and add a few notes to describe each scene.

Planning your novel

Describing your story's main scenes can help with writing either a short story or a novel. Novelists may outline their chapters like this, in which case it is called a chapter synopsis. Mapping the plot in advance, keeps them on track once they start writing, although they may still make changes as they go along.

A famous example

Katherine Paterson's *Bridge to Terabithia* is a realistic fiction story that tells of the friendship between misfits Jess and Leslie. Here are the storyboard captions:

1. Jess wakes up early every morning to go jogging. He wants to be the fastest runner in the fourth grade.

2. Leslie's family moves into the old farmhouse next door. Jess and Leslie meet.

3. School starts, and Leslie and Jess are in the same class. At recess, Leslie races the boys and wins.

4. Jess and Leslie become friends and create a secret, imaginary kingdom on the far side of a creek in the woods near their homes. They call their kingdom Terabithia.

5. Jess gets Leslie her puppy, which they call Prince Terrien, for Christmas.

6. Leslie goes to church with Jess' family for Easter. Afterward, she, Jess, and his little sister May Belle talk about the story of Jesus.

7. It rains all week. There's so much water that Jess is afraid to cross the swollen creek to Terabithia. He doesn't tell Leslie because he knows she'd never be afraid.

8. A teacher asks Jess to come to a museum for the day. Jess goes along. It's still raining, and he doesn't want to cross to Terabithia.

9. When Jess gets home, he finds out that Leslie fell in the creek on the way to Terabithia and died.

10. Jess goes to Terabithia and grieves. May Belle follows him but gets scared crossing Jess' makeshift bridge. Jess has to rescue her.

11. Leslie's family moves away.

12. Jess builds a new bridge and leads May Belle into Terabithia.

Novels versus short stories

Bridge to Terabithia is a short novel, but with its single storyline and two main characters, it could also work well as a much shorter story. Once you know your own story's main scenes, you can decide if there is scope to expand each one into a chapter and thus create a novel, or if a short story structure would work best for your narrative. Both forms may contain equally big ideas, but while a short story distills them into a few telling scenes, the novel elaborates and shows them off in different settings and circumstances.

Expanding a short story

If you choose the novel option (and they can be easier to write than a finely tuned short story), then try to think of each chapter as a mini-story inside a larger story. Each chapter will have a beginning, middle, and end, but it will also carry the story forward. There will be much more space to develop both main and supporting characters and to reveal them to readers in different moods and situations. There will also be more scope for building suspense with action scenes, plot twists, and subplots. Dividing the story into chapters also helps to build suspense and draw readers in ever more deeply. Remember, a novel is not a short story made longer, but a short story made deeper.

Now it's your turn

Weave a story web

If you are struggling with your story map, try this exercise. Give yourself 20 minutes. In the center of a large piece of paper, draw a picture of your hero in a circle. Think about his or her problems. Then draw six spokes extending from your "hero circle." At the end of each spoke, write down one fact or idea that the central image makes you think of. When you have six thoughts, write a sentence or two explaining them one by one. Extend each spoke and write down the next thought that comes to you. Work around all the spokes in this way. If there's room on the paper, extend the spokes to create a third set of thoughts. Take a break. Then look over the web. Has it made your character's situation become clearer?

BAIT THE HOOK

You have planned your plot and are ready to start telling your own story. Focus on your hero—how will you make readers care about him or her?

Hooking your readers

The opening scene may show your hero's usual life just before a crisis strikes and makes things worse. Or you could dive straight into the crisis and backtrack later to explain the situation. Many stories also begin with the meeting of two central characters, which sets off the drama of their adventures together.

Kate DiCamillo's *Because of Winn-Dixie* has a humorous opening:

> *My name is India Opal Buloni, and last summer my daddy, the preacher, sent me to the store for a box of macaroni-and-cheese, some white rice, and two tomatoes and I came back with a dog. … He was a big dog. And ugly. And he looked like he was having a real good time.*
>
> Kate DiCamillo, *Because of Winn-Dixie*

The reader is instantly hooked, wanting to know how the main character came to bring the dog home. Her honest speech lets the reader know she will tell a good story, and the dog seems to love adventure.

TIPS AND TECHNIQUES

Hook your readers with your first sentence and paragraph. Make your opening mysterious, dramatic, or funny. Put the best of your writing skills to work and make your opening grab readers. Write it and rewrite it. Read it aloud to hear how the words flow together.

GETTING STARTED | SETTING THE SCENE | CHARACTERS | VIEWPOINT

Create a mystery

In *Absolutely Normal Chaos*, Sharon Creech begins with a letter. This is instantly enticing because most people secretly like the chance to read someone else's letters. By the fourth sentence, there is also a mystery, and readers can guess that the story is going to be amusing:

> *Dear Mr Birkway,*
>
> *Here it is: my summer diary. As you can see, I got a little carried away. The problem is this, though. I don't want you to read it. I really mean it. I just wanted you to know I did it. I didn't want you to think I was one of those kids who says, "Oh yeah, I did it, but I lost it/my dog ate it/my little brother dropped it in the toilet." But please Pleeeassse Don't Read It! How was I to know that all this stuff was going to happen this summer?*
>
> Sharon Creech, *Absolutely Normal Chaos*

In *Maniac Magee*, Jerry Spinelli begins the story as if it were a legend. This is enticing because it makes the reader instantly wonder what could be true and what could be false.

> *They say Maniac Magee was born in a dump. They say his stomach was a cereal box and his heart a sofa spring. They say he kept an eight-inch cockroach on a leash and that rats stood guard over him while he slept. They say if you knew he was coming and you sprinkled salt on the ground and he ran over it, within two or three blocks he would be as slow as everybody else. They say. What's true, what's myth? It's hard to know.*
>
> Jerry Spinelli, *Maniac Magee*

BUILD THE SUSPENSE

It's all too easy for a story to sag after a good opening. Now is the time to turn up the tension. Think of your hero's problems. How can you make them worse? Stir and complicate. Put your characters under constant pressure.

Out of the frying pan

Sometimes characters pick the wrong solution for their problems and find they are worse off than when they began. In Christopher Paul Curtis' *Bud, Not Buddy*, motherless Bud runs away in search of his father. He struggles to survive on the city streets.

Multiple threats

In *The Edge* by Alan Gibbons, Danny and Cathy escape from Chris Kane and find refuge with Danny's grandparents. But Chris Kane sets out to track them down, and Danny's grandfather has a racist dislike of Danny. And finally, there are the racist bullies at Danny's new school. All these threats intertwine and build toward a nail-biting climax.

Now it's your turn

Problems escalator

Brainstorm your main character's problems again. First write his or her flaws or weaknesses at the top of the page. In the bottom lefthand corner, start drawing a staircase. The bottom step will be your hero's problem at the story's beginning. Write it on the step. Draw a second step and write the hero's next problem (make it a little bit worse) on that step. Repeat the process up the page for as long as you can. Use your hero's flaws and weaknesses to give you ideas. Give yourself two minutes for each step and write only your first thoughts.

Add a time challenge

In *Walk Two Moons,* the main character, Salamanca, goes on a car trip with her grandparents. They have only a week to journey across America, but they intend to visit all the places that Salamanca's mother had stopped at on an earlier trip. Salamanca is desperate to reach her mother's final destination in time for her birthday. Near the end, Grandma is bitten by a snake. Will they reach their destination in time?

Have a false happy ending

In *The Illustrated Mum*, Star's father, whom she has never met before, returns and wants to rescue both Star and Dolphin from their disturbed mother. Things seem to be looking up. But just when she has the chance to escape, Dolphin finds she is jealous of Star's good luck and decides to stay.

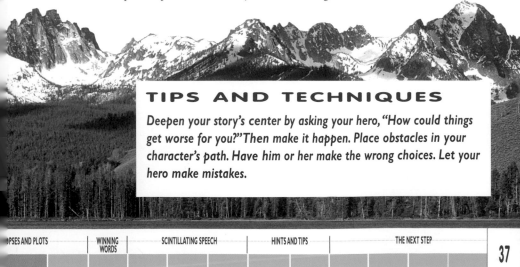

TIPS AND TECHNIQUES

Deepen your story's center by asking your hero, "How could things get worse for you?" Then make it happen. Place obstacles in your character's path. Have him or her make the wrong choices. Let your hero make mistakes.

In the last part of your story, the hero's problems must reach a dramatic climax. After this, the hero's problems will be solved— or at least changed for the better.

Bring your tale to a climax

Happily-ever-after endings should be avoided in realistic fiction. Instead, aim for an upbeat ending where things work out hopefully rather than perfectly.

Suggest new beginnings

At the start of *Harriet the Spy*, Harriet doesn't really care about her friends and is more interested in writing in her notebook and keeping up on her spy route. But at the end of the story, she realizes the importance of friendship and how much she needs Janie and Sport.

She looked up at Sport and Janie. They didn't look angry. They were just waiting for her to finish. She continued: "Now that things are back to normal I can get some real work done." She slammed the book and stood up. All three of them turned then and walked along the river.

Louise Fitzhugh,
Harriet the Spy

ug the heartstrings

t the end of Phyllis Reynolds Naylor's *Shiloh*, Marty has earned his dog from Judd Travers and rings Shiloh home with him forever:

> *I'm thinking how nothing is as simple as you guess—not right or wrong, not Judd Travers, not even me or this dog I got here. But the good part is I saved Shiloh and opened my eyes some. Now that ain't bad for eleven.*

Phyllis Reynolds Naylor, *Shiloh*

ad endings

ad endings are those that:

fizzle out because you've run out of ideas

fail to show how the characters have changed

are too grim and leave the readers with no hope

MAKE YOUR WORDS WORK

Realistic fiction needs sharp, vivid writing about how people behave. Use language that is true to life. Every word counts.

Write with bite

Keep descriptive passages short. Think of snapshot images. If possible, make your description reveal something about the characters. In this example from *Walk Two Moons*, Sharon Creech shows us Salamanca's deep sense of loss:

Use vivid imagery

To help readers stand in the characters' shoes, writers often use poetic comparisons or "word pictures." In *The Illustrated Mum*, Dolphin doesn't know how she will cope when Star leaves. She uses a striking metaphor to describe how empty she feels, calling herself "a balloon girl with a trailing string lost in the emptiness of the sky."

> *Just over a year ago, my father plucked me up like a weed and took me and all our belongings (no, that is not true—he did not bring the chestnut tree or the willow or the maple or the hayloft).*
>
> Sharon Creech, *Walk Two Moons*

Write from the heart

In *Bridge to Terabithia*, Jess can't hide how Leslie's death has affected his life:

> *"Leslie, were you scared? Did you know you were dying? Were you scared like me?" A picture of Leslie being sucked into the cold water flashed into his brain. "C'mon Prince Terrien. We must make a funeral wreath for the queen."*
>
> Katherine Paterson, *Bridge to Terabithia*

More vivid imagery

In *Joey Pigza Swallowed the Key*, Jack Gantos uses a metaphor and simile to describe a feeling that everyone can understand. When Joey puts on his first new medication patch, he feels himself "winding down like I was on a swing that was slowly stopping."

Make action scenes active

Action scenes need crisp phrases that focus on what is happening. In *Maniac Magee*, Jeffrey runs through town on the line that divides East End from West End, each side waiting for him. Notice the number of verbs Spinelli uses. What do you think this adds to the scene?

Cars beeped at him, drivers hollered, but he never flinched. The Cobras kept right along with him on their side of the street. So did a bunch of East Enders on their side. … Both sides were calling for him to come over. And then they were calling at each other, then yelling, then cursing. But nobody stepped off a curb, everybody kept moving north, an ugly, snarling black-and-white escort for the kid in the middle.

Jerry Spinelli, *Maniac Magee*

USE DRAMATIC DIALOGUE

Dialogue lets readers hear what your characters have to say in their own words. If well-written, dialogue brings characters to life. Conversations between characters are also a good way to give information while pushing the story forward.

Create realistic dialogue

The best way to learn how people talk is to eavesdrop. But don't simply listen for snippets of gossip. Pay attention to the actual words used. Tune in to conversations over lunch, in the street, or on the bus. Look out for interesting expressions or particular patterns of speech. Watch people's body language, too. What do they do when they're telling someone a secret they promised to keep? Look, listen, and absorb.

GETTING STARTED | SETTING THE SCENE | CHARACTERS | VIEWPOINT

Now it's your turn

Break the bad news

Your best friend urgently needs you on a mission, but your parents say you can't go. Write the conversation as you break the news to your friend. Do you end up arguing? Don't rely on dialogue tags like "yelled" or "cried" to show the mood. Show the feelings in the words the characters use. Then revise the argument and take out any unnecessary tags ("he said" or "she said"). Cut down the words to the bare bones. This is the essential skill of editing your own work.

Following conventions

The way dialogue is written down follows conventions. It is usual to start a new paragraph with every new speaker. What they say is enclosed in quotation marks, followed by "he said" or "she said" to indicate the speaker. Speech tags may be left out if we know who is speaking, or they may be placed in the middle of some speech lines to give the impression of the pauses in real conversation. The example on the right is taken from *Because of Winn-Dixie* by Kate DiCamillo. Notice how the author makes the conversation easy to follow.

"Is it Halloween?" Otis asked when I handed him the candy.
"No," I said. "Why?"
"Well, you're giving me candy."
"It's just a gift," I told him. "For today."
"Oh," said Otis. He unwrapped the Littmus Lozenge and put it in his mouth. And after a minute tears started rolling down his face. "Thank you," he said.
"Do you like it?" I asked him. He nodded his head. "It tastes good, but it also tastes a little bit like being in jail."

Kate DiCamillo, *Because of Winn-Dixie*

TIPS AND TECHNIQUES

Dialogue gives the impression of real speech; it doesn't copy it word for word.

USE DRAMATIC DIALOGUE

Conversations between characters can be used to push the story forward and quickly explain things about the speakers, the story, or other characters.

Show what characters are like

If you are writing from a limited viewpoint (third or first person), the only way you can reveal supporting characters' opinions directly is by using dialogue. Even a first-person narrator may not reveal everything about his or her thoughts and feelings in the narrative. It is only when we hear them talking with others in dialogue that we learn more.

In *The Illustrated Mum*, narrator Dolphin presents herself as a lonely, dreamy girl who often has to mother Marigold through her bad times. But at school, where she is used to being shunned and ridiculed by Kayleigh and Yvonne, we see a much tougher side:

"Her mum!" said Yvonne.

They all sniggered. My fists clenched.

"Did you see her tattoos?" said Kayleigh.

"All over her! My mum says tattoos are dead common," said Yvonne.

"Your mum's just jealous of my mum because she's a great fat lump like you," I said, and shoved her hard in her wobbly stomach.

"Um, you punched her!" said Kayleigh.

"Yeah, and I'll punch you too,"
I said, and I hit her hard, right on the chin.

Then I marched out of the toilets, the other girls scattering in alarm.

Jacqueline Wilson, *The Illustrated Mum*

Now it's your turn

With or without?

We are told a lot in the exchange between Yvonne, Kayleigh, and Dolphin (previous page). Go through the excerpt and list every piece of information. Then rewrite the scene without any dialogue but include all the information and convey the feelings of all the characters. Read your version and the original aloud. Which sounds better?

TIPS AND TECHNIQUES

When writing dialogue, stick to "he said" or "she said" for your speech tags most of the time. But you can use words like "asked," "cried," or "whispered" to create some variety or to suit the situation in your story.

Now it's your turn

Spill the beans

Write a conversation between your hero and a friend. The hero should slowly reveal something important—something he or she is ashamed of or angry about. The friend must coax it out. Convey both characters' feelings. Find small ways to make their speech distinctive. Perhaps one uses an expression frequently.

Dialogue may reveal the speakers' ages, how well they have been educated, and if they come from a particular place or culture. In other words, they will not all speak like you.

Go easy on the slang

In realistic stories, it is tempting to use current styles of speech— *puh-lease, whatever, I was like...,* and so on—as well as the latest slang words. Be careful. This will date your writing, and your story will lose its freshness faster than a carton of milk. It is better to use plain English, or to suggest current slang by coming up with your own original ways to use words and your own expressions.

TIPS AND TECHNIQUES

Watch out! Today's "cool" words are tomorrow's has-beens.

Who's Who?

In the following examples, the dialogue reveals who the characters are and gives an insight into their personalities. This is all accomplished in the space of just a few sentences, as words are used sparingly and powerfully:

Child and parent

"Where's Winn-Dixie?" I shouted. "I forgot about him. I was just thinking about the party and … I forgot about protecting him from the thunder."

"Now, Opal," the preacher said, "he's probably right out in the yard, hiding underneath a chair. Come on, you and I will go look."

Kate DiCamillo, *Because of Winn-Dixie*

Boys in class

"Yeh! People with babies have to be totally unhinged." It was Sajjid, as usual, who put the point over most coherently. "I mean, they stroll round all day with real ones tucked under their arms that keep bawling and messing and having to have their bums wiped—"

"Not just their bums!" interrupted Henry. … "Grotesque!"

Anne Fine, *Flour Babies*

A regional accent

"Might be the car-bust-er-ator," he said, "or maybe not." He tapped a few hoses. "Might be these dang snakes." "Oh, my," the woman said. "Snakes? In my engine?" Gramps waggled a hose. "This here is what I call a snake," he said.

Sharon Creech, *Walk Two Moons*

A language barrier

"N-O." He wrote the letters with the plastic tube in the air. "Do you understand me? Nyet. Nein. Non. No."

Madame spread her hands. "If you are good at something and you do not do it, then you are dead inside."

Laurence Yep, *Angelfish*

BEAT WRITER'S BLOCK

Learning to write has ups and downs, and even famous writers get stuck. This is called writer's block. If you have been sticking to the writer's golden rule (sitting down and writing regularly), then you already have some weapons to fight writer's block. Here are some of the most common causes and cures.

Ignore your internal critic

It's your internal critic, the Story Saboteur, that tells you that everything you write is no good. Do not listen. Do some timed brainstorming right away, such as describing the best day you ever had. Write down just first, unedited thoughts.

No ideas

Another cause for writer's block is thinking you have nothing to say. Again, if you write and practice often, you will trigger ideas. You have learned how to search for story ideas. If nothing else, you can scan the lost-and-found columns in your local newspaper and imagine the stories behind the ads. Or repeat any of the exercises in this book.

Now it's your turn

Positive thinking

Write a note to yourself in your writing notebook: "Writing is magic, but it's not always easy." Brainstorm for five minutes, listing all the things you find hard about writing. Now list all the things you love about writing. Look over the problems. Can they be fixed with more time, practice, and reading? Is learning to write more important to you than the problems? If the answer is yes, your stories will get written.

Cope with criticism

No one enjoys rejection or criticism, but they are important parts of learning to be a writer. If you invite someone to read your stories, you have to prepare yourself for negative comments. As you develop your writing skills, you will add faith in yourself and your storytelling skills. Try to see criticism as a chance to make your story better.

Thinking everyone is a better writer

This is a common trap into which even experienced writers fall. How good a writer you become is up to you and how hard you want to work at it. Only you can tell your stories, and every new one is an addition to the treasure trove of human stories. Read other writers' works to help you improve. Be grateful for their guidance, but don't envy them.

TIPS AND TECHNIQUES

To avoid writer's block:
* *Keep reading.*
* *Always carry a notebook and write down interesting ideas.*
* *Keep a diary and set yourself a daily word target, maybe 300 words.*
* *Watch an episode of your favorite TV show, then rewrite it as a story.*
* *Give your brain a break—clean your room, walk the dog. Ideas come anytime, anywhere.*
* *Do more reading.*

When writer's block leaves you stuck midstory, it usually means there has not been enough planning. Don't panic. If your story seems stalled, there are ways to get it moving again.

Shake up your thoughts

If your story has stalled, look at your synopsis again. Read it carefully. Have you wandered off the point and sent your hero down a dead end? If so, step into your hero's shoes and ask, "How am I feeling? What's my next move?" Brainstorm for 10 minutes.

Group practice

Writing is a lonely occupation. Sometimes talking your ideas through can remove an obstacle. Brainstorm with friends. Tell them the story so far. Then let them take turns to say what happens next.

Now it's your turn

Correspondence course

Make your hero your pen pal. Write him or
her letters or e-mails. Write his or her
replies to you. Compete to see who can
tell the best story. Maybe you are jealous
over some talent of your hero. Maybe
you boast about something you can do to
make up for this. Start building a real
relationship. Brilliant ideas may emerge.

More character building

If your main character still isn't coming
to life, write a brief description of him
or her, then ask your friends to add
their ideas. Give each person two
minutes. Don't worry about writing
complete sentences. Look over the
results. Have you learned something
new about your character?

TIPS AND TECHNIQUES

*Don't forget to play the what-if game when stories stall. Ask
questions about your character and story. What if your hero
finds out that his father isn't his real father? What if your hero
discovers a close friend has been lying to him or her? How
would your story change and move ahead?*

TAKE THE NEXT STEP

Completing your first story is a wonderful achievement, regardless of whether it is a short story or a full novel. You have set your imagination free and shown you can write. Put your first story away in your desk drawer and think about what comes next.

Another story?

While you were writing the first story, did some new ideas start simmering in your mind? Did you make a note of them? If so, look them over, repeat some of the exercises to help develop your ideas, and start a new story!

How about a sequel?

When thinking about your next work, ask yourself: Is there more to tell about the characters I have created? Can I write a sequel and further develop the story? This is what happened to Jack Gantos (right) and his character Joey Pigza. One book turned into three (a trilogy) as the writer explored Joey's problems in more ways. Sometimes a minor character might clamor to have his or her own story told.

How about a series?

Paula Danziger's Amber Brown is a good example of a character who keeps growing. One book simply wasn't big enough to include everything that happens to her. Each book about Amber is a complete story. But all the details of her life, her friends, her school, and her parents' divorce carry on from book to book. The author must really know and love the character to write a series.

Case study

Megan McDonald developed the Judy Moody series by remembering her own growing up. She says that being the youngest of five girls often put her in a bad mood. When she recalls some moody moment, it inspires a new story.

A writer's conundrum

If you have created a character who insists on having his or her own series, you need to think about whether that character will grow up and change from book to book. Some readers like their heroes to stay exactly the same in each book. What do you think? Would this be appropriate for realistic fiction, or should your hero evolve from book to book?

Every writer says the same thing: Writing is hard work; you must stick with it through thick and thin, even when writing is the last thing you feel like doing.

So if it's not easy, why do writers write?

• They write because they feel they must.

• They write to tell a story that must be told.

• They write because they believe that nothing is more important than stories.

• They write because it's the thing they most want to do.

Jack Gantos

Author Jack Gantos says that the biggest hurdle is getting started. He also says that writers of all ages have this problem because they think nothing interesting happens to them. He believes that keeping a diary is good way for a fiction writer to start. Gantos began his writing career with the *Rotten Ralph* picture books. These were inspired by the antics of his naughty cat.

Jacqueline Wilson

Jacqueline Wilson has been a professional writer since she was 17, when she went to work for a teenage magazine called *Jackie*. But when she was 9, she wrote a story about a family with problems, and she has been writing stories like this ever since. She writes with an appealing mix of sorrow and humor. Her advice is to keep a diary, which will help you to get into a daily writing habit.

Anne Fine

Anne Fine's most famous book, titled *Madame Doubtfire*, became the popular film *Mrs. Doubtfire*. It deals with parental separation and divorce. Most of her stories explore serious family issues in a humorous way. Her advice: "Write the book you would most like to read."

Michael Morpurgo

To break writer's block, Michael Morpurgo (author of *Private Peaceful*) says, "If you get stuck—and I do often—go for a long, long walk, tell yourself the story aloud." He also says he gets his ideas from his memories and interests. He does a lot of historical research, too. He believes that writers must find their own way of working, and that there is no right or wrong way. His advice: "Tell it from the heart, as you feel your story, as you see it."

Judy Blume

This award-winning author (left) says that "ideas come from everywhere—memories of my own life, incidents in my children's lives, what I see and hear and read—and most of all, from my imagination." She has used her own experiences in many of her books. Her family life was a lot like the family in *Starring Sally J. Freedman as Herself*. Fudge in *Tales of a Fourth Grade Nothing* is based on her own son Larry when he was a toddler, although Larry did not swallow a turtle as Fudge does.

After your story has been resting in your desk for a month, take it out and have a read through it. You will be able to see your work with fresh eyes and spot flaws more easily.

Editing

Reading your work aloud will help you to simplify rambling sentences and correct dialogue that doesn't flow. Cut out all unnecessary adjectives and adverbs, and extra words like "very" and "really." This will instantly make your writing crisper. Once you have cut down the number of words, decide how well the story works. Does it have a satisfying end? Has your hero resolved the conflict in the best possible way? When your story is as good as can be, write it out again or type it up on a computer. This is your manuscript.

Think of a title

It is important to think of a good title—something intriguing and eye-catching. Think about some titles you know and like.

Be professional

If you have a computer, you can type up your manuscript and give it a professional presentation. Manuscripts should always be printed on one side of white paper, with wide margins and double spacing. Pages should be numbered, and new chapters should start on a new page. You can also include your title as a header on the top of each page. At the front, you should have a title page with your name, address, telephone number, and e-mail address on it. Repeat this information on the last page.

TIPS AND TECHNIQUES

Whether you type up your story on a computer or do it by hand, always make a copy before you give it to anyone to read.

Make your own book

If your school has its own computer lab, you could use it to publish your own story or to make a story anthology (collection) with your friends. A computer will let you choose your own font (print style) or justify the text (making even margins like a professionally printed page). When you have typed and saved your story to a file, you can edit it quickly with the spelling and grammar checker, or move sections of your story around using the cut-and-paste tool, which saves a lot of rewriting. Having your story on a computer file also means you can print a copy whenever you need one.

Case study

Anne Fine writes all her stories in soft pencil that is easy to erase. She ends up surrounded by eraser rubbings. Even when she has finished a story, she does lots of revisions and editing. It takes her about a year to write a children's book.

The next step is to find an audience for your realistic fiction. Family members or classmates may be receptive. Or you may want to share your work through a Web site, magazine, or publishing house.

Find places to publish your story

There are several magazines and a number of writing Web sites that accept stories and novel chapters from young fantasy writers. Some give writing advice. Several run regular competitions. Each site has its own rules about submitting work to them, so make sure you read them carefully before you send in a story. Here are some more ideas:

- Send stories to your school newspaper. If your school doesn't have a newspaper, start your own with like-minded friends.

- Keep your eyes peeled when reading your local newspaper or magazines. They might be running writing competitions you could enter.

- Check with local museums and colleges. Some run creative-writing workshops during school holidays.

Case study

Sometimes struggling writers are writing the wrong thing. Megan McDonald, creator of Judy Moody, wanted to be a poet until her writing teacher told her to go home and rip up all her poems. He told her she was a prose writer. After looking up what "prose" meant, she went on to prove him right.

TIPS AND TECHNIQUES

Every published book you have ever read was likely rewritten over and over before it was accepted for publication.

Begin a writing club

Starting a writing club or workshop group and exchanging stories is a great way of getting your realistic-fiction story out there. It will also get you used to criticism from others, which will prove invaluable in learning how to write. Your local library might be kind enough to provide a space for such a club.

Find a book publisher

Secure any submission with a staple or paper clip and always enclose a short letter (explaining what you have sent) and a stamped, self-addressed envelope for the story's return. Study the market and find out which publishers are most likely to publish realistic fiction. Addresses of publishers and information about whether they accept submissions can be found in writers' handbooks. Bear in mind that manuscripts that haven't been asked for or paid for by a publisher—unsolicited submissions—are rarely published.

Writer's tip

If your story is rejected by an editor, see it as a chance to make it better. Try again, and remember that having your work published is wonderful, but it is not the only thing. Being able to make up a story is a gift, so why not give yours to someone you love? Read it to a younger brother or sister. Tell it to your grandmother. Find your audience.

Some last words

All stories show us the truth about ourselves, but realistic stories give us the chance to think about some difficult issues. They help us put on other people's shoes and see what their lives might be like.

Every new story is a journey, both for the writer and the reader. At the end of the journey, both are changed, hopefully for the better. This is the real magic of writing realistic fiction.

GLOSSARY

back story—the history of characters and events that happened before the story begins

chapter synopsis—an outline that describes briefly what happens in each chapter

cliffhanger—ending a chapter or scene of a story at a nail-biting moment

dramatic irony—when the reader knows something the characters don't

editing—removing all unnecessary words from your story, correcting errors, and rewriting the text until the story is the best it can be

editor—the person at a publishing house who finds new books to publish and advises authors on how to improve their stories by telling them what needs to be added or cut

first-person viewpoint—a viewpoint that allows a single character to tell the story as if he or she had written it; readers feel as if that character is talking directly to them; for example "It was July when I left for Timbuktu. Just the thought of going back there made my heart sing."

foreshadowing—dropping hints of coming events or dangers that are essential to the outcome of the story

genre—a particular type of fiction, such as fantasy, historical, adventure, mystery, science, or realistic

manuscript—your story when it is written down, either typed or by hand

metaphor—calling a man "a mouse" is a metaphor, a word picture; from it we learn in one word that the man is timid or weak, not that he is actually a mouse

motivation—the reason why a character does something

narrative—the telling of a story

omniscient viewpoint—an all-seeing narrator that sees all the characters and tells readers how they are acting and feeling

plot—the sequence of events that drives a story forward; the problems that the hero must resolve

point of view (POV)—the eyes through which a story is told

publisher—a person or company who pays for an author's manuscript to be printed as a book and who distributes and sells that book

sequel—a story that carries an existing one forward

simile—saying something is like something else, a word picture, such as "clouds like frayed lace"

synopsis—a short summary that describes what a story is about and introduces the main characters

third-person viewpoint—a viewpoint that describes the events of the story through a single character's eyes, such as "Jem's heart leapt in his throat. He'd been dreading this moment for months."

unsolicited submission—a manuscript that is sent to a publisher without being requested; these submissions usually end up in the "slush pile," where they may wait a long time to be read

writer's block—when writers think they can no longer write or have used up all their ideas

FURTHER INFORMATION

Visit your local libraries and make friends with the librarians. They can direct you to useful sources of information, including magazines that publish young people's short fiction. You can learn your craft and read great stories at the same time. Librarians will also know if any published authors are scheduled to speak in your area.

Many authors visit schools and offer writing workshops. Ask your teacher to invite a favorite author to speak at your school.

On the Web

For more information on writing *Realistic Fiction Stories*, use FactHound to track down Web sites related to this book.
1. Go to *www.facthound.com*
2. Type in a search word related to this book or this book ID: 0756516420
3. Click on the *Fetch It* button.
FactHound will find the best Web sites for you.

Read more realistic fiction

Almond, David. *Kit's Wilderness*. New York: Delacorte Press, 2000.

Cleary, Beverly. *Dear Mr. Henshaw*. New York: Marrow, 1983.

Cormier, Robert. *Frenchtown Summer*. New York: Delacorte Press, 1999.

Creech, Sharon. *Walk Two Moons*. New York: HarperCollins, 1994.

Danziger, Paula. *The Cat Ate My Gymsuit*. New York: Delacorte Press, 1974.

DiCamillo, Kate. *Because of Winn-Dixie*. Cambridge, Mass.: Candlewick Press, 2000.

Fine, Anne. *Flour Babies*. Boston: Little, Brown, 1994.

Gantos, Jack. *Joey Pigza Swallowed the Key*. New York: Farrar, Straus, and Giroux, 2000.

Hobbs, Valerie. *Charlie's Run*. New York: Frances Foster Books, 2000.

Hobbs, Valerie. *Defiance*. New York: Farrar, Straus, and Giroux, 2005.

Kehret, Peg. *My Brother Made Me Do It*. New York: Pocket Books, 2000.

Littman, Sarah. *Confessions of a Closet Catholic*. New York: Dutton Children's Books, 2005.

Morpurgo, Michael. *Private Peaceful*. New York: Scholastic Press, 2004.

Myers, Walter Dean. *Scorpions*. New York: Harper & Row, 1988.

Paterson, Katherine. *Bridge to Terabithia*. New York: HarperCollins, 1977.

Paterson, Katherine. *The Great Gilly Hopkins*. New York: Crowell, 1978.

Vail, Rachel. *Daring to Be Abigail*. New York: Orchard Books, 1996.

Voight, Cynthia. *Dicey's Song*. New York: Atheneum, 1982.

Woods, Jacqueline. *From the Notebooks of Melanin Sun*. New York: Blue Sky Press, 1995.

Read all the Write Your Own books:

Write Your Own Adventure Story
ISBN: 0-7565-1638-2

Write Your Own Fantasy Story
ISBN: 0-7565-1639-0

Write Your Own Historical Fiction Story
ISBN: 0-7565-1640-4

Write Your Own Mystery Story
ISBN: 0-7565-1641-2

Write Your Own Realistic Fiction Story
ISBN: 0-7565-1642-0

Write Your Own Science Fiction Story
ISBN: 0-7565-1643-9

Picture Credits. Alamy: 10t, 18-19 all, 21 all, 35, 48 all. Andrew Holbrooke/Corbis: 12b. Banana Stock: 33. BrandXPictures: 28, 41t, 61. Catherine Karnow/Corbis: 5. C. Willhelm/Photex/zefa/Corbis: 42t. Comstock: 32, 40. Corbis RF: 14-15 all, 16t, 17t, 22-23 all 24-25 all, 38 t, 44-45 all, 54 all. Corel: 34-35c, 39. Creatas: 8 all, 9r, 12t, 20t, 26-27 all, 29 all 46-47 all, 48-49c, 49r, 56-57 all, 58-59 all, 60. LFPA: 13. fotosearch: 4, 6-7 all, 30 all, 36-37 all, 42b, 43, 50-51 all. Getty images: 52-53c, 53b. Karen Huntt/Corbis: 1, 38b. Mika/zefa/Corbis: 41b. Rex Features: 8-9c, 10c, 11, 17l, 20b, 52b, 55. Saverkin Alexsander/ITAR-TASS/Corbis: 30-31c. Every effort has been made to contact copyright holders of any material reproduced in this book. Any omissions will be rectified in subsequent printings if notice is given to the publishers.